NO BS BIZ BOOK

VOL. 1

© 2023 No BS Biz Co. Ltd.

nobsbizco@gmail.com

https://nobsbizco.mykajabi.com

Editing & Formatting by The Infinite Power of You Inc.

Visit:

https://amanda-rose.mykajabi.com/book-creation

Cover by Daniel McCutcheon

For Cover Art Inquiries, Contact

mccutcheondan@gmail.com

1st Edition

Table of Contents

CUT THE SHIT AND BUILD A BUSINESS YOU LOVE

Erin Nettere

Take Leaps of Faith

Have you ever heard the sound clip on TikTok or Instagram that says, "Do you ever just look at someone and think… what is going on inside their head?" That's what I hear when I look back at my previous self.

I spent a lot of my early life searching for the *right thing*, the *right place*, the *right person*. I was *CONFIDENT*, as all 20-year-olds are, that I was doing it right. But that 20-year-old had no idea who she was, she had no idea that the "norms" of society were not for her, and she had no idea of what was waiting for her outside of her little people-pleasing, happy-go-lucky, vanilla as fuck bubble.

I lived life *way* too mature for my early 20's; I graduated college, got married, and got a proper job all by the time I was 23 years old. Unfortunately, it took me another four years until

I woke up and realized I was living a life that I had created but hadn't chosen. I followed the path that society deems as "the way" to go about life, and then I realized what bullshit that was.

In the years that followed, I got a divorce and spent the rest of my 20s getting to know myself. I like to say I lived my 20's in reverse, mature and married at 22, young dumb, and having fun at 29. The years between 27-30 really showed me a lot and also how little I truly know about myself, the world, the universe, and, well… everything else. By the time my 30s hit, it was time to really figure it out.

Let's start this part by saying I had no clue what I was doing or the ways in which my life was about to change. I took a *GIANT* leap of faith; I quit my job, sold everything I owned in life, hopped on a plane to Bali, and started a new chapter. This is one of the top 3 best decisions I have ever made. By the time I was headed to Bali, I had also met this guy, who was different, and he was kinda great. When he said he was going to come with me to Bali, for some reason, I agreed. He spent a week with me, and I stayed for another month or so without him, but that week told me everything I needed to know about him. We're now married, and that was the number 1 best decision of my life.

In Bali, I explored, meeting other travelers and locals, enjoying their history, traditions, foods, culture, and incredibly beautiful Island. This time of my life was beautiful, it was amazing, it was life-changing, and simultaneously it was hard! Anyone who tells you traveling solo to the other side of the world, where you know no one, you don't know the customs, the intricacies of the language, or have someone else to say, "Hey, I saw a place back there, let's try it for dinner!" is lying to you. It's hard, it's exhausting, but it's transformative in the best possible way. I highly recommend it for the right person whose ready and brave enough to find themselves, but I don't recommend it for everyone.

As my Bali trip was coming to an end, I was on the phone with Carl, my then-boyfriend, buying a van in Florida while I was in Ubud, at 2 A.M. Yes, next up in this wild ride of life I bought a van, sight unseen by me. Carl had driven it on my behalf. I purchased it with the intention of heading back to the States and converting it into a camper to live out the *#vanlife* experience.

So, that's what I did. I headed back to the States, slept off the jet lag, and got to work on *Wanda* the van. Being back stateside and building out a campervan without a job made me feel two ways. First and foremost, not exactly abundant in the finances department. Secondly, it made me feel rather directionless in terms of what would fulfill me mentally and emotionally work-wise.

One thing I knew was that there was no going back to the corporate world. Anything that required me to be at a certain place at a certain time every day was not an option. I started looking for remote jobs. In 2017 the market was not plush with work-from-home opportunities. Every virtual assistant company out there had thousands of applicants for $10-an-hour jobs that had a 6-month wait list before the job was even available. All of that sounded as terrible as the soul-sucking corporate job.

I really had no idea what to do, and I just kept Googling "remote work jobs." I remember finding a list, and I was so overwhelmed and frustrated at this point that I was determined to find my next job on that list. I scanned it for a while and decided that a social media manager sounded alright, so I went with it. That's literally how I decided to start a social media management business, picking it from a list and deciding I could figure it out. I had no passion for it then and no understanding of the position whatsoever, but hey, now I'm over five years in, and I think it worked out pretty well.

Then it was time to start a business. How exactly do you do that? "Ummm… hey Google, we're about to be besties." I Googled all the legal stuff and bought a course called "Freedom Junkies" to teach me the rest. It taught me everything I needed to know about social media, creating a social media business, and getting started with my new venture. At the time, it cost $800, and I was terrified to make that investment, but it was the first investment I made that made me realize how important it is to invest in yourself as you grow a business and in life in general. Yes, I could have Googled everything in that course, but had I chosen to do that, would I have actually known *what* to Google? No way. The course was well worth the investment.

No BS Biz Tip # 1

My first big lesson in business was clear: **in order to get anywhere you need to invest in**

yourself. Sometimes that feels like taking a massive gamble on yourself, as well as the person who is going to be developing you, but it's so necessary to trust yourself and trust your gut.

I technically launched my business, and by launch, I mean started a Facebook and Instagram page and posted to my friends and family that I was open for business. As I was scrolling on Facebook one day, I saw a post from a friend I had gone to high school with, Hayley. She was now living in LA, running her own esthetician business. She was now a Therapeutic Skin Coach and happened to be looking for a social media manager. "Oh my god, perfect! This is my first shot!" I thought, and I went for it! I instantly messaged her, saying I had just started a social media management business and would love to talk with her. We jumped on a call a few days later, and the next thing I knew, I had my first client! It was so exciting and encouraging, but I still had no idea if I could actually do this.

We started, and I put everything I learned into that account. I went to Google and YouTube constantly to keep learning how to achieve the goals we'd set for that account. That account was my baby, my pride and joy, and let me tell you, that account defined the social media business I would eventually create. Scrolling her feed was the most soothing, self-care-inducing, beautiful part of my day. I suddenly saw posts every day about self-care, personal growth, development, manifesting, and female-owned businesses crushing it. It wasn't that I was becoming a *work-a-holic*, I truly enjoyed doing the work on her account. I wanted to be there, and I wanted to see what was being posted by others in that circle.

As business went on, I took on more clients outside of the esthetician, self-care, and mindful niche. They were great because I needed to pay the bills, but they weren't the Therapeutic Skin Coach. I gave them a lot of my heart and soul, but they didn't get it all like that account did.

No BS Biz Tip #2

Another theme that kept coming up with clients was that the majority of people who were willing to take a chance on me were other female entrepreneurs. Mainly ones who were more established, who had been at it for a few more years than I was. One who stood out and took a chance on me was a woman named Sarah. She loved building her businesses as well as helping others build their businesses. I remember a conversation she and I had where she said, "I love to support up-and-coming women-owned businesses because I remember being in their shoes at one point, doing whatever it takes to make it work." This stood out and is one lesson I have remembered along my journey. **Remember where you came from and give others the chance you would have dreamt of when you were in their shoes.**

No BS Biz Tip #3

The first three years of my business were filled with a lot of figuring it out and not doing it the easy way. **If I could go back in time, I would have hired a coach so much sooner, even if it wasn't the same caliber of coach I would work with today. Someone a few steps ahead of me who charged a price I could afford at the time would have helped speed things along so much faster.** But live and learn, and there was a lot of that happening during that time, *living and learning.*

I got to do the digital nomad thing between living the *#vanlife* while creating my *#laptoplifestyle* and taking a few big international trips, one being a 6-week solo trip around Vietnam. That was quite an experience, working with a 12-hour time difference from my clients. The focused work hours without any interruption from the other side of the world was so nice, but the middle-of-the-night meetings were rough. Nonetheless, I'm glad I did that then. Now, with my multiple screens and perfect office setup, I have no idea how I got all the work done from a 13-inch laptop.

There came a time when I just knew it was time to take my business to another level. I was tired of the 4-5 accounts bringing in just $2-3k per month. It was a lot of work for not much money.

No BS Biz Tip #4

Then, just like with all things in life, as soon as you say, "I think I need something new," the universe delivers. Within a few weeks, I didn't even realize it, but I was shopping the coaches that were being brought to me through participating in a few free trainings. In the end, I went with a coach who specialized in building social media agencies, and I'm glad I did because it was the right decision at the time. It was a terrifying investment of $11K, which made that $800 course look like nothing, but it was 100%

worth it. I worked with her for about a year, and one of the first lessons I learned was to **know my worth**. At the time, I was still treating myself and charging like that same social media manager who was just so happy to have a client and didn't know if she could do it. I was three years in at that time. I knew I could do it, and I knew I was pretty darn good at it. It was time to level up and show the clients why I was worth 3-times what I had been charging.

No BS Biz Tip #5

This coach's motto was "**massive imperfect action**," and from day 1 with her, I started doing that **every day**. I let go of clients who wouldn't work with my new business model, I let go of clients that I realized I was losing money on, and I created space for the right clients to come along. But before the new clients came along, can we just remember I was making $2-3k per month, and I had to cut over $1K in monthly income by letting the wrong clientele go to make that happen? Talk about a trust fall! It was time to do the work, put the lessons into action, and make the next chapter happen. And it did. I cut over $1K in revenue between 3 clients, and suddenly I had one client sign for 3.5k a month… *wait, what?*! Never in my life had I had someone pay me over $1,000 a month, and suddenly I have one client paying $3.5k a month! I knew then that this was going to work!

Now the fancy coaches don't stop you from learning through the school of life, but they do help you move past those lessons faster, and they help you avoid the ones they can. I still had a lot of learning to do, but the lessons came fast, and they helped me uplevel one right after another that year. That year as I was bringing on higher-paying clients, changing the way I work, and refining my services. I also started building a team. In June, I hired my first two team members, and by mid-July, I was out of commission with Covid for five weeks. I was lucky, I was never hospitalized, but it was at a time when the variant was very strong and really did a number on some people. Ariana, my new social media assistant, kept my business running during this time, and without her, I honestly don't know what I would have done. Being out like I was made me realize very quickly that I absolutely had found the right person for my business, and she is still with me today. She is now the social media director of *Soultivity Studio.* She runs my team and the day-to-day operations of the business.

When my time was up with my first coach, something was telling me it was time to move on to someone new. I now had a solid foundation for running and growing the social media agency, and it was time to expand in a way that felt right. I wanted to create a coaching program of my own that would allow entrepreneurs to learn how to do social media that would truly help their businesses when they are at a stage when paying for a full agency is out of reach.

Then, of course, by that manifestation magic, I asked, and the teacher appeared. My next coach was hosting a free workshop the following week. I attended, and by the time we jumped on a call, the words out of my mouth were, "Take my money!" After almost a year with this coach, I now have online offerings at affordable price points. I get to share my message that social media can be mindful, it can be an act of self-care, and I get to coach people to social media success while still offering done-for-you services for businesses that are at that level. My impact is so much greater in the past two years after working with incredibly talented coaches, and it's partially due to their impact on me, partially my drive to get it done, and partially that investment that makes it all come together.

No BS Biz Tip # 6

I have learned the power that comes with investing in yourself, *and* **I have also learned that the investment is worthless unless you put in time and effort.** I'm over here building it from the bottom up, and in order to get the success from the investment, I need to show up, I need to put in the work, I need to surround myself with the right people, and I need to strive to be 1% better every day. The impact and the ripple effect that my business has is a mark I am proud to leave on this planet.

No BS Biz Tip # 7

I have learned I need to continue to dream and expand my vision of what is possible. **Without a vision of what is next and the impact I can make, there's no future beyond my current reality.** When I dream, I can find passion and purpose. I can find ways to make each day meaningful and move toward something better for me and all those around me.

Six years ago, I was working a job I hated. Now I get to wake up every day and make people's dreams come true. I have six people who work with me currently, and for three of them, I am their sole employer. My business allows four people, including myself, to fully live their lives in the way that they want to live.

I get to help entrepreneurs reach their goals, grow their businesses, and watch their dreams become reality. It is amazing, and through enabling everyone else to live their dreams, my dreams continue to expand and also become a reality. I get to help people at all stages of business take the next steps. I'm able to put the same faith in my team members that other entrepreneurs put in me when I was just starting out. I have the coolest, most amazing, best job in the world, and I am so grateful for everything I have created, and it's all because I took a leap of faith… or 5. I invested in myself, I did the work, and I continue to show up for myself and all the dreamers out there that know they are here for something more than the "normal" path through life.

Amy Dabrush Lewis

ENTREPRENEURSHIP Can be a Mindfuck!

"Take the leap," they said.

"Just go for it," they said.

"You know most new businesses fail, right?" they said.

"Follow your heart, and your path will reveal itself," they said.

"Others will say you're crazy," they said, and you will wonder if you are, in fact, crazy.

"It won't be easy," they said, "but it will be worth it."

Sound familiar? As an entrepreneur, especially a first-generation entrepreneur, the mindfuck can be incredible. Everyone has opinions about what you're about to do, and they sure aren't afraid to share them. There is so much information out there, and if you're anything like I was when I started, you've got a bunch of what I call "head trash" that must be dealt with. More doubts bubble up to the surface with each step up, and the opinions of others never stop berating you, making it so that you would *LOVE* to be able to serve from the shadows, with confidence.

You see, with a giving heart and burning desire to serve comes a duty, a responsibility, and an obligation to put yourself out there; to share your new-thought leadership, to tell your story, and to teach the life-altering transformational steps you possess. Most heart-centered entrepreneurs have something in common that holds them back, keeps them playing small, and from ever really achieving their visionary goals and dreams, which means never really serving the soulmate clients that are searching for them day-in and day-out.

No BS Biz Tip #1

Why is this? Why do heart-centered leaders suffer and struggle to have the income and impact they desire and deserve? **The Main culprit of this struggle and strife in heart-**

centered, visionary leaders, cultural creatives, and social entrepreneurs is not wanting to be seen.

If you're anything like my younger entrepreneurial self, you long for a *cloak of invisibility*. You want to be the superhero that flies through the night, transforming lives quietly behind the scenes. Putting yourself out there is an overwhelming, and maybe even terrifying, proposition, because:

- *What will people think?*
- *What if my thought leadership looks stupid?*
- *What if nobody wants to hear what I have to say?*
- *What if they belittle my purpose and passion?*
- *What if I can't really help anyone?*

What if, what if, what if…

While being invisible can be appealing, it is important to remember that putting yourself out there and being visible is crucial for building relationships and achieving success in business. It can be scary, but it is necessary for growth and reaching your goals. Otherwise, you keep your gifts locked away, and your tribe suffers. If they cannot find you, they can't receive your amazing gifts that could change their lives.

As an entrepreneur, it is important to have a clear understanding of your target market and to communicate effectively with them. This includes understanding their needs, desires, and pain points, then effectively communicating how your product or service can address those. Building a strong personal brand and having a solid marketing strategy can also help increase your visibility and attract customers. Additionally, networking and building relationships with other professionals in your industry can also help increase your visibility and credibility. It is equally as important to have a clear, deep, and meaningful why so that you stay the course when the going gets tough.

Having a clear sense of purpose, or knowing your *why,* is crucial for entrepreneurs, as it provides motivation and direction during the inevitable challenges that come with starting and running a business. When the going gets tough, a strong sense of purpose can help keep you focused on your goals and remind you of the greater vision and mission of your business. Furthermore, having a clear why can also help attract customers and partners who share your vision and values. It also allows you to stay true to yourself and to your values so that you make decisions aligned with them.

No BS Biz Tip #2

Tweak your "what ifs." Imagine what life will be like when you intentionally craft your leadership based on serving your clients. It is important for entrepreneurs to identify their unique selling point (USP), or differentiators, and communicate them effectively to potential customers and clients. This statement succinctly communicates the value and benefits of your product or service. It's important that it is clear, concise, and compelling enough to make people want to know more.

Having a clear understanding of your unique selling point and being able to effectively communicate it can help set your business apart from the competition and attract potential customers and clients. Additionally, it can help guide decision-making and ensure that all aspects of the business are aligned with the overall vision and values of the company. It's also important to note that it is important to be constantly testing and refining your USP statement, as your business and the market may change over time.

When you create an intentional strategic plan that allows you to show up as the best version of yourself, confidently and competently, you will find that it is easy for your soulmate client to easily find you. This can increase the likelihood that your ideal soulmate clients will find you and want to work with you. Additionally, aligning your actions with your values and goals makes you feel more fulfilled and satisfied in your work, which can lead to a more positive and successful professional experience.

Imagine what life will be like when you know how you want to show up and no longer need that cloak of invisibility. Imagine what it feels like when you realize it's *your vibe* that attracts your tribe, and they *are* searching...for YOU! Now, embody that feeling. You will likely feel more confident and self-assured. You can be true to yourself and attract people who align with your values and goals when you're acting from this energetic space. You may form deeper, more authentic connections with others and be able to build a supportive community around you. This sense of belonging and connection can lead to greater happiness and fulfillment. Additionally, by being true to yourself, you can find people who share the same values and interests, which will lead to a more positive and fulfilling life.

When you have a clear and intentional action plan inspired and aligned with your core values, you feel a sense of purpose and fulfillment in your daily actions, even when the results you seek aren't immediate. You will feel more motivated and focused and be able to prioritize tasks and activities that align with your values. This can lead to a greater sense of satisfaction and well-being and can help you to achieve your goals and live a more meaningful life.

When you shed the invisibility cloak and proudly share the gift that you are with those who need you now, and you step into the leadership role, the love and trust factor both you and your soulmate client need to connect emerges. Confidently share your unique gifts and talents with the world because it's how you can make a positive impact on the lives of others. When you help others in need of your specific skills and knowledge, it will bring a sense of fulfillment and purpose to your life. Additionally, by sharing your new-thought leadership and knowledge with others, you can establish yourself as an expert in your field and build a reputation as a trusted authority. This increases the likelihood that your ideal clients will find and want to work with you. When both you and your clients trust each other, it creates a foundation for a successful and fulfilling professional relationship.

When you accept and step into your greatness and commit to serving your soulmate client, you can make a powerful impact on the lives of others. You'll be able to use your skills, knowledge, and expertise to help others achieve their goals and aspirations. By committing to serving your clients in achieving their desired transformation, you'll be able to provide them with an exceptional level of value, which can increase the likelihood of building long-term, successful relationships with them.

I know it can be scary, but isn't it scarier to think about the people waiting for you who need your solution and won't be able to find it because your fear got in the way? It is natural to feel fear when facing a new or difficult task, but it is important to remember that fear should not prevent you from acting. The people who need your solution are counting on you, and by acknowledging your fear and acting in spite of it, you can make a positive impact on their lives. It is important to remember that fear is a normal part of the human experience, and it is possible to work through it and accomplish your goals.

I invite you to step into your power, share your thought-led leadership, and serve from the heart. Stepping into your power as an entrepreneur means embracing your unique skills, talents, and experiences, and then using them to achieve your goals and make an impact in your industry. This can include providing valuable insights and expertise through writing, speaking, or other forms of content creation. Additionally, it's important to adopt the mindset of serving others, putting the needs of your customers and clients first, and approaching your business with a mindset of making a positive impact.

Sharing your expertise and serving from the heart can help establish you as a leader in your industry, build trust and credibility with your target audience, and ultimately attract more customers and clients. It's important to be authentic and true to yourself when sharing your insights and serving others. This will help you build a loyal customer base who trust and believe in your business.

No BS Biz Tip #3

Create simple and effective success habits to build a strong foundation for your business and set yourself up for success. Some examples of simple, effective success habits that entrepreneurs can implement include:

1. **Setting clear, specific, and measurable goals:** This will help you stay focused and motivated as you work towards achieving them.

2. **Creating a daily routine:** This can include tasks such as setting priorities for the day, reviewing your goals, and working on specific projects.

3. **Staying organized:** This can include using a calendar, to-do list, or project management tool to keep track of tasks and deadlines.

4. **Staying focused:** This can include setting aside specific times during the day for focused work and minimizing distractions, such as turning off notifications on your phone or using a distraction-blocking app.

5. **Staying healthy:** This can include things like getting enough sleep, eating well, and making time for regular exercise.

6. **Continuous learning:** this can include reading, attending webinars or workshops, and networking with other entrepreneurs.

These habits can help you stay on track, stay productive, and make steady progress toward your goals. Additionally, it's important to remember that success habits are not one-time things; they are something that you should be working on continuously and adjusting as per the need.

No BS Biz Tip #4

Self-care is an important aspect of being an entrepreneur, as it helps to maintain physical and mental well-being and prevent burnout. Incorporating self-care success habits into your daily routine can help you stay energized and focused and improve your overall quality of life. Some ways to implement self-care for entrepreneurs are:

1. **Limiting added sugar and eating whole foods:** Consuming a diet that is high in added sugar can contribute to health problems such as diabetes and obesity. Eating whole foods, on the other hand, can provide the body with essential nutrients and improve overall health.

2. **Getting quality 7-8 hours of sleep:** Getting enough sleep is crucial for maintaining physical and mental health and preventing burnout.

3. **Hydration:** Drinking 8 glasses of water per day can help to keep the body hydrated and improve overall health.

4. **Move at least 15 minutes per day:** Regular physical activity can help to improve cardiovascular health, boost energy levels, and reduce stress.

5. **Stress reduction:** Taking 5 minutes each day to practice stress-reducing techniques such as deep breathing, meditation, or yoga can help to reduce feelings of stress and improve overall well-being.

It's important to note that incorporating these habits into your daily routine requires consistency and discipline, but over time they easily become part of your daily routine and improve your overall well-being.

As an entrepreneur, identifying and committing to personal values can help to guide decision-making and establish a sense of purpose for the business. Aligning actions with those values can also help to build trust and credibility with customers, employees, and other stakeholders. Additionally, living by your values can also help to attract like-minded individuals and create a positive company culture.

For example, if one of your values is environmental sustainability, then you might make choices in your business that reflect that value, such as using eco-friendly materials or implementing recycling programs. This can not only make you feel good about the impact of your business on the environment but also help you attract customers who share that value.

As another example, let's say that one of your values is to help others, and your goal is to start a non-profit organization. In this case, even if you are afraid of public speaking or fundraising, you will be more likely to do these things anyway because you know that your values and goals are more important than your fear.

No BS Biz Tip #5

Having a clear set of values can also make it easier to navigate ethical dilemmas that may arise in the course of running your business. When faced with a difficult decision, entrepreneurs can refer to their values to help guide their actions. Defining your values, beliefs, and goals is an important step for long-term success as an entrepreneur and in life in general. It helps provide direction and purpose and can serve as a compass for decision-making. When values, beliefs, and goals are clearly defined, it makes it easier to stay focused and aligned with what's important to you, which can lead to more meaningful and fulfilling experiences.

Overall, defining your values, beliefs, and goals is a necessary step for long-term success as an entrepreneur and in life; it provides direction, purpose, and clear communication for your vision. When you focus on your values, beliefs, and goals, it can help to shift your perspective and reduce the impact of fear. By keeping your values, beliefs, and goals at the forefront of your mind, you can remind yourself of what is truly important to you and what you are working towards. This can give you the motivation and determination to push through any fears or obstacles that may arise.

Focusing on values, beliefs, and goals helps to reduce the impact of fear and increases your resilience. When you are working towards something that is important to you and aligns with your values, it can give you a sense of fulfillment and motivation, which can help to overcome the fear. Before you know it, you'll be willing to shout your message from the highest mountain peak because your mission, vision, and values will be aligned. You will feel drawn to action.

When your values, beliefs, and goals are aligned while you are working towards something that is important to you, it can give you a sense of passion and purpose. This can inspire you to act and be more confident in expressing your message to others. Add to that clarity about your mission, vision, and values. You will feel more confident about your message, and it will be more likely for you to take bold actions to share it. With an aligned mission, vision, and values, you will be more motivated to take risks and strive to be more visible in expressing your message. This can lead to greater impact and fulfillment in your business and personal life.

In summary, when your mission, vision, and values are aligned, it can give you a sense of passion and purpose that can inspire you to take action and be more visible in sharing your message. It can also help you to overcome fears and insecurities, leading to greater impact and fulfillment.

No BS Biz Tip #6

In the end, yes, entrepreneurship sure can be a mind fuck, but with the right tools, you can reduce the mind fuckery of entrepreneurship. To do just that, I suggest you take these steps:

1. **Develop a clear and specific business plan:** Having a clear plan in place can help reduce

uncertainty and provide a roadmap for achieving your goals.

2. **Set realistic expectations:** Entrepreneurship can be challenging, and it's important to have realistic expectations about the time and effort required to be successful.

3. **Stay organized and prioritize:** Managing your time and tasks effectively can help reduce stress and ensure that you stay on track.

4. **Build a support network:** Surrounding yourself with people who can provide guidance, mentorship, and encouragement can help you navigate the ups and downs of entrepreneurship.

5. **Practice self-care:** Taking care of yourself both physically and mentally is important for maintaining your energy and focus.

6. **Learn to deal with stress and uncertainty:** Entrepreneurship can be stressful, and it's

important to develop strategies for dealing with stress and uncertainty, such as meditation, exercise, or therapy.

7. **Stay flexible and adaptable:** Being open to change and willing to pivot, when necessary, can help you navigate the challenges of entrepreneurship and increase your chances of success.

8. **Don't be afraid to ask for help:** Seek advice and mentorship from experienced entrepreneurs, and don't be afraid to ask for help when you need it.

If you need a hand, or aren't sure where to start, grab a cuppa your favorite beverage and reach out to me!

Kaeli Mulvaney-Courtois

"Mechanic" Entrepreneur

"I have no right to be in a book written by entrepreneurs!" I'm sure we all think that… at least, I hope some other people do too. Just like my mind, this chapter may jump around, but that's the natural way restless minds work, and eventually, we'll get there. There are "face" entrepreneurs who are bravely in the public eye whenever possible, but self-promotion has never been easy for me. I'm more of the "mechanic" entrepreneur; in the background, quietly making things work and then making them work better.

I grew up being always on the go. I was in swimming, baseball, gymnastics, choirs, and pretty much anything else I could try. I was outside with friends, creating new games and languages, constantly using my imagination, and exploring new worlds. As a church kid, I did youth group, presented for the younger children, sang in the choir, served during service, and volunteered at camps and events. I volunteered at the museum, spending days living and exploring historical lives. I was in music camps, art camps, and spent a massive amount of time with my family, playing, creating, doing puzzles, and all around just having fun. I also got some phenomenal financial knowledge starting at a young age because my dad was on the ball!

My days were so full that I would leave one activity early to arrive at another one late. I loved it! I've always tended to bite off an awful lot. Sometimes it's been a lot to contend with; however, it makes for great stories and varied experiences that I'm extremely grateful for.

In kindergarten, my teacher reported that I "parallel played." Basically, I would sit nearby other kids and do my own thing while they did theirs. I joke that my sister was created solely to help me with this, but to be honest, I still do it. Throughout elementary school, I brought my creativity into every project I could. When we had a project to sell a pyramid, I built a massive Bristol board shell and created a Lego interior. When I was done, you could open the pyramid and see inside of it. This project came complete with a scroll that professed the multitude of my pyramid's benefits with as many puns as possible included.

Even as a kid, I was self-aware and had no problem taking responsibility. I've always had an outlook in life of, "This is my problem. How do I solve it?" An example is, generally, when I get sick, I lose hearing in one or both of my ears. Because of this, I learned to partially read lips and body language; to take the bits of communication that I got and puzzle them together until they made sense.

No BS Biz Tip #1

I started working when I was 14 because I wanted to. My first official job was at a chip wagon. I worked with a lady who despised working with "kids," which to her was anyone under 18 years of age. Her bias was so severe that when the 18-year-old cook accidentally touched the grill, with only the tip of his thumb, for less than a second, he earned her immediate attention and first aid treatment, but in contrast, when I had fryer grease splashed on my face and loudly exclaimed, "Ow!" I was told that I was unprofessional. **These early trials, and the people who cause them, stick with us and can help us push to create our lives intentionally so that we no longer put up with other people's bullshit.**

My creativity sometimes clashed with the leadership abilities of the blunt and impatient being I am. Our high school music teacher frequently complained that we took too long to warm up for band. I may have pointed out that if he got there when we did, we'd be ready when he wanted. He didn't want to come earlier, so I got a key. Problem solved.

No BS Biz Tips #2 & 3

If you want someone to solve a problem, make it their problem. Also, **if you want a disinterested person who's in power to solve a problem, literally hand them an easy solution**. I received many responsibilities and leadership roles in response to acting in this manner. What can I say? *I like to fix things.*

After a lengthy decision period after high school, I attended Carleton University for Aerospace Avionics Engineering. I volunteered in various organizations and was chosen to manage the student-run engineers' convenience store & lounge. Even though the boss was a micromanager with a blind side to details, I managed to make improvements to the environment and keep it running. I worked behind the scenes while we were closed to avoid having to spend hours convincing the "boss" that the things I was doing were needed.

I later discovered that when the committee was trying to decide who deserved the award for Leo's because "no one really did much this year," my significant other had put them in their place about my contributions. It's possible that if I'd had more self-confidence or just mounds of ego, I'd have been spared some pain in this and so many other situations, but the truth is that overall, I just don't have the patience for any of that. After all, I'm a *mechanic entrepreneur*, remember?

I graduated as one of four in my program when, despite that "job guarantee," the industry was shifting from needing engineers to needing technicians. I spent an entire year applying to jobs across Canada for everything from minimum wage work to Avionics Engineering positions. I was too qualified to be considered a serious candidate for some jobs and not experienced enough to compete for the engineering ones. I didn't even get the chance to bomb in an interview. Sometimes "no news" makes you question your abilities. But the show must go on, and if engineering was out, I decided I would pursue another interest: *teaching*.

I was the last class at Nipissing University to go through the 1-year program. With a military significant other and an impending move to an unknown job market, I got not only my Intermediate/Senior qualifications for math and physics as well as my Primary and Junior qualifications, giving me the ability to work grades JK-12.

I moved to a town where the only socially acceptable reason to be there was to have a connection to the military. We bought a house, and I learned that I'm amazing at concrete parging, a process so wacky I could write a comedy about it. I submitted to both the public and Catholic school boards for better chances to get hired, and then I started as a supply teacher. Remember I said I was very musical? Due to my experience, I landed a maternity leave position as an instrumental music teacher. I worked hard with the kids and eventually had a contract as well as a band I could take to Kiwanis to compete the next year! …And then I was transferred.

Environment affects a lot. I was moved from an area that understood the value of the arts and a staff that worked as a team despite the grade they taught to an area that thought little of the arts and a staff that functioned in cliques. I tried my best to function there and even took a group of absolutely amazing grade 5 students to compete in *Destination Imagination Globals.* It was an experience I will never forget. But despite that high, I couldn't stay squished forever.

Go back to school? *Why not?* I wasn't accepted to the Sheridan Musical Theatre program, but I discovered they had another program that taught musical theatre and technical production basics. An amazing combination of my creative and engineering sides! I had planned to use the time at school as professional development for teaching, but I ended up loving simply tapping into my creative side without squishing into other's boxes. I attended Randolph College after Sheridan, where a lot of my time was online due to COVID.

I stretched my leadership skills in both programs, setting up Google Drives that kept track of literally every important piece of information and making sure every student had access...*I'm a teacher, ok!?* I pitched my business services to Randolph and met with them, but they have a rule about current and recent students being blocked from partnership.

No BS Biz Tip #4

So, why am I still talking about my life when this book's supposed to be about entrepreneurs when almost every job I've made money for has been "regular"? Great question! As a kid, I was creating and distributing a class newspaper. I also used to make and sell crafts like plastic canvas creations. I've always had some sort of side hustle going on, be it making and selling things or providing various services. It's always been who I am. I'm constantly moving and looking for new challenges. There always comes a point where I want to surpass the job expectations or where I feel held back by the structure and rules. **Busting the bubbles is a core entrepreneurial personality trait.**

Entrepreneurship is both the easiest and hardest way to make money. It's "easier" to increase income because you don't have to pass an interview, and you get to make your own expansion decisions. But every new client, post, and sales pitch is like a new interview, and owning your own business is not always a guaranteed paycheck. Being your own boss can also be overwhelming. Freedom is appealing, but in the beginning, you tend to spend *WAY* more time juggling the seemingly endless to-do list.

Lately, I've split my time between "secure" jobs to pay bills and entrepreneurial endeavors when possible. This last summer, I finally got in to be assessed for mental health and discovered that I have ADHD, OCD, General and Social Anxiety, as well as a handful of other fun things. It's amazing what insight you can find when you have a specific direction to look. Past and present troubles now make total sense, and we're working on building on the coping mechanisms I have from growing up. I wouldn't have been diagnosed, however, had I listened to my doctor and followed the "Well, you can hold a job, so you're fine" train of thought. Yes, I have skills gained from figuring out how to survive school situations, but being able to research specifics has allowed me to be even more self-aware and add to my arsenal.

Keeping that in mind, my entrepreneurial past is hard to follow because I have multiple interests and tend to hyper-focus on a project, then drop it the minute I finish it because I'm bored. Social media promotion? I hate speaking to the "void," and I am not a huge fan of "mindless" office tasks. The idea of posting and not having any sort of discussion or interaction afterward makes me wonder what the point is. Logically, I know that people are getting substantial takeaways and are just not interacting, heck, I do that, but things that aren't stimulating are very difficult for me to continue doing consistently.

Let's add recent events. My appendix burst, resulting in surgery, and having to defer the first semester at Randolph, shifting my plans by months. My ten-year relationship ended while I was there, so I moved back in with my parents to rent from them when COVID sent us all online. An accident that totaled my car forced me to buy a new one and added to the debt I'd already amassed with school. During COVID, because I was in school, I wasn't considered "able to get a job," so I was denied Unemployment Insurance and the rest of my return-to-in-person learning had to go on my credit card.

That resulted in me working three jobs for other people as well as pursuing my own entrepreneurial projects, trying to pay my monthly bills and make a dent in my debt. Where did all that financial knowledge I learned when I was a kid go? It's still there, and it's helping me out. You can only manage the money you have, so I do what I can with what I have now as I'm working my way back up to the financial freedom I had when I was a teenager.

As with most entrepreneurs, I struggle with doing things for *ME*. I excel at helping others improve *THEIR* things. I work best behind the scenes. This may make finding new clients difficult for me if I don't have enough people to spread the word, but that doesn't touch my abilities and awesomeness with what I do. I guide others. I have such a deep feeling of obligation, loyalty, and caring that I go above and beyond for people who want to improve, no matter the subject. My multiple interests and job experiences mean I can help in a variety of subjects.

Due to my struggles, I can relate to others and have a ton of different methods for coping. I've known since I was young that I must follow my moods. If I feel like working, I better do it now because later it's going to take longer when I don't feel like it. This self-awareness allows me to notice when I need music or absolute silence, and my ADHD ability to love a method for months and then have it not work the next morning means that I have a library of tested methods for others to explore.

No BS Biz Tip #5

Being self-aware makes you better at making decisions based on your current state. The more you know about yourself, the more aware you become of others. For example, knowing that when you're tired you tend to get a little snippy or have trouble understanding more complicated concepts helps you to see it in others so you can be more patient and understanding. Share what you know about yourself with others so they can be more understanding toward you. If I'm having a day where my patience is low, I'll let the class know that they should gently point it out if I snap over something that didn't really need it.

No BS Biz Tip #6

Put your unique spin on what you do. In school, I would pair a project I didn't like with something I did. If we had to write an essay, I'd write it on a topic I loved to talk about, or I'd make a video or song to show I knew something. Knowing yourself helps you to "fit in" while still being yourself. This is the basis of my *METHOD for Your MADNESS* courses and workbook.

No BS Biz Tip #7

Work smarter, not harder. This one almost everyone is aware of, but few implement it. Step back from your problem, get ALL the details, not just the ones you think you need, and then figure out what the smart way is for you.

No BS Biz Tip #8

If you're reading this book, I bet you've heard all about mindset and positive perspectives. Take time to dwell on whatever has gone wrong, but then assess it rationally, put it into perspective, and figure out how to move on from there. **It's easier said than done, but being able to acknowledge and work through your feelings so that you're not avoiding them and then assess where you are and where you want to be, is a skill that will get you through pretty much anything.**

I hope that my story has shown you that no matter what you go through, you can rise. It may be a quick fix or years of struggle, but if you're moving in the right direction, you're succeeding.

Becky Shapiro

Don't Limit Yourself

When looking for divine inspiration to start this chapter, I was reminded of the title of the book. So, thanks to the spirit, you get the most no BS version of me, the most authentic me to date. As you read through my story, notice what jumps out at you. *What really resonates with you?* Learn from my mistakes, so you will make fewer on your no BS Biz journey!

My childhood was pretty normal, so we're going to skip ahead. Due to the positive experiences that I had growing up, I became an elementary teacher after college. I was excited that I was going to make a difference in kids' lives!

Teaching is complicated, frustrating, and rewarding all at the same time, which is why so many women stick with it. Shit… it's definitely not for the pay! It's certainly not for the respect either; educators are treated like children by the administration and their district. There's a lot of other stress involved coming from deadlines, paperwork, behavior issues, and disrespectful parents.

So, why did I stay in the teaching field for over 21 years? Part of it had to do with my relationships with my co-workers, if you were lucky enough to be on a team of cooperative, helpful peers, who had your back, that was motivating! The other part of it had to do with truly making a difference in students' lives, whether it was academically, mentally, or emotionally. Some kids had it rough at home, and I was the only-fucking-ray of sunshine in their lives. My mission as a teacher was to guide children on how to think for and advocate for themselves.

The truth is that I didn't intend to stay in education that long. In my mid-thirties, I fell in love and got married for the first time. It all happened rather quickly, and we had a child right away. I thought we were soulmates.

My husband happened to be a Reiki Master, which is a specific type of energy healing practitioner. I had never heard of energy work before, but I had an open mind to it. He also soon became an instructor of another modality called *Quantum Touch*. He used this healing technique on me while I was pregnant to realign my hips and send energy to our baby.

After understanding the incredible benefits of this powerful technique, I also became a Quantum Touch practitioner. Together, we dreamed of starting our own natural healing business. We actually did start it; it just didn't go anywhere. I continued working full-time as a teacher while my husband left his job and got things going.

My hope was to eventually be able to quit teaching, which I no longer felt passionate about. Shortly after getting the business started, we also became Foot Reflexologists, so we had another service we could offer clients. Though we had a website and Facebook page and were trying to advertise, our business wasn't going anywhere. Most people have never heard of either energy healing or reflexology, especially where we lived! Adding to that, we also had no expertise in how to promote ourselves.

As the business slowly fizzled out, so did our marriage. We couldn't agree on much, and because we were both afraid of conflict, too much resentment had built up. Our relationship eventually ended, and the hardest part was reconciling the fact we couldn't be together as a family anymore.

By that time, I wanted out of teaching. It was sucking the fucking life out of me. But at this point, I was stuck. As a single mom, I couldn't venture out on my own and risk not being able to pay my bills and support my child. You have to understand, I didn't trust the

Universe at the time to provide me with what I needed.

A few years later, I was doing okay on my own. Teaching was still stressful, but my bills were paid. Then divine intervention urged me to contact a friend and start a romantic relationship. After several years, we tied the knot right as the pandemic hit in 2020, one of the last marriages allowed in the city for months.

Fast forward six months. Teaching had become incredibly stressful for me during the pandemic, but not because of the virus itself. I had never felt so out of control in my life with the constant changes to guidelines from the city and district. I was having anxiety about the uncertainty of the future.

I resigned two months into the school year after 21 years at the same school. This was not something I ever expected myself to do. I was so overwhelmed and believed the school district wasn't doing enough to support its staff. Their only interest seemed to lie with the students. I thought, "Fuck that. I'm too old to put up with this shit anymore."

Looking back, I now know it was the Universe kicking me in the ass to make changes. It was shouting at me to move on. Teaching was no longer my path. I was meant for something else.

For the first time in over two decades, I chose to put myself first. I immediately jumped into helping at a Wellness Center. I used my energy healing and reflexology skills to work on clients. Eventually, we added breathwork lessons. I became a certified yoga instructor and started teaching classes.

Though my life was way less stressful now, I realized this wouldn't be enough for me. I wanted to work with people more holistically. I wanted them to have the skills to take home with them that they needed to be able to release their emotions and beliefs, which are what cause our physical issues.

In late 2021, I discovered I didn't know who I was anymore. I'd lost myself in all my different roles: as a mother, wife, daughter, and teacher. I felt like I was lost. I had lost *me*.

No BS Biz Tip #1

Always taking care of others for several decades had caused me to forget what my needs and wants were. Or that they were just as worthy as everyone else's needs and wants for me to make time for. I believe there are a lot of other women out there who have forgotten who they are in the busyness of taking care of others. **It's key to our well-being that we discover our wants and needs and prioritize ourselves.**

Over the next year, I took a lot of classes and learned a lot of helpful techniques that brought me back to myself. They made me feel whole again. As I pushed myself through this journey, with little assistance from others, I realized how helpful guidance would have been.

I developed an online membership program for moms who want to add joy back into their lives. A space for women who are ready to prioritize themselves again but don't know where to start. I also started my own spiritual awakening. As I was taking better care of myself and going within more, parts of me were starting to open and expand.

By this point, I had been working with some of my spiritual gifts for almost a decade, but I never understood what they were. I didn't know I had psychic abilities. I began working with my gifts, expanding them. I allowed myself to play and explore. I asked for guidance from my divine team once I knew how to speak with them, and they taught me so much. *All I had to do was ask.* I didn't know what was to become of these abilities. I just knew it was bringing more joy into my life.

In 2022, it was no longer a fit for me to work at the Wellness Center. I believed it was holding me back. I wasn't venturing out on my own because I was playing it safe. I was "needed" there, even if only part-time. Being there was a helpful stepping stone on my journey, and I am grateful for the experience. I worked with many moms there, gaining a deeper understanding of why they don't put themselves first and why they feel that they cannot make time for self-care. This led me to discover the mom guilt, which is a real thing. It prevents most women from taking care of themselves or putting themselves first.

I provide the techniques for healing and releasing the mom guilt, and my clients move forward at their aligned pace to rediscover their joy. So, after leaving the wellness center, finally, I was on my own. *Oh, shit!* It was time to become a full-time entrepreneur.

No BS Biz Tip #2

When I started promoting myself the previous year, I had no idea what I was doing. I had so much to learn, especially about technology. I quickly realized I was going to need some mentoring, coaching. I followed different people who resonated with me, taking advantage of their free advice and content. But… **you only get what you pay for! Investing in coaching is investing in yourself.** Plus, as a Mind-Body-Spirit Coach myself, I understand the importance of accountability. **Someone who can motivate you to stay on track and motivate you to take the action you're afraid to take, is invaluable.**

No BS Biz Tip #3

I needed someone to push me to take risks and put myself out there in a way I hadn't yet. I learned that, for me, working with the same business coach is only helpful for a while. Eventually, I need to move on to someone who can inspire and motivate me in a different way.

Someone who can pull something new out of me. Otherwise, stagnation occurs. **Don't be afraid to let someone go, be it a client or a coach.**

We alone are responsible for our growth and expansion. Along the way, I've come to understand how important mindset is. How incredibly powerful it is to work with your mental self-care. After working with so many clients, I had an epiphany: *our thoughts cause our feelings which cause our physical issues.* So, even though you may be exercising and eating right, if you're not improving what's going on in your mind, then you're still going to feel like shit. This has become a huge focal point in my content and how I help others move forward.

As I continued to go deeper within and work with my spiritual abilities, I learned some of my strengths and weaknesses. This was important; because if we are leading with weakness, it's going to show. I had to let go of feeling inadequate because of a weakness. *I let that shit go.* Use your strengths to shine with them, and use your weaknesses to showcase your humanity. People are relieved to know you're a fallible human, just like they are, and it will create a connection with prospects and clients.

Making time for myself to go within and connect above has brought me so much abundance in the last year. I know it sounds counterintuitive. *How can spending less time on business-related activities improve your revenue?* But, when you are only ever in "go, go, go mode" and neglecting your needs, you aren't really offering up your best to anyone. When you're in that state, you are working from a place of lack and a space of exhaustion. This energy radiates out, affecting everything you touch, including your business.

When your business lights you the fuck up, though, you will move with passion and joy. You will attract the right clients. As I've made daily time for my energy work and made my connection routine non-negotiable, it's transformed my life. It's brought me peace, clarity, creativity, trust, and a deepening of my faith. It's allowed me to perceive that there is so much more I'm meant to do than I could have ever imagined!

The more I make space in my day to work with my spiritual team, the faster my gifts strengthen and expand. My efforts are constantly being rewarded with new insights, skills, answers, and activations. The more I practice what's bringing me joy and share it with others, the more light I spread.

To get to this point, I had to get the fuck over holding myself back. I wasn't allowing myself to share what had been building for me with the world. I had been keeping what I'd been practicing to myself for fear that some people might reject me. Since then, I've come to see that this is a limiting belief many others hold too.

No BS Biz Tip #4

I learned that the more I allowed the world to see the real me, the authentic self I'd been hiding for a decade, the more supported I felt. This took courage to put myself out there in such a vulnerable way, but I will never regret it. I knew I would continue to be held back, stuck, until I faced my fears. **It doesn't matter what your business is, whether it's spiritual or not, we all have fears and doubts we need to push through.** Taking those scary-ass steps toward your future, no matter how small, are so worth it. For me, taking that huge leap forward, despite the fears and doubts, only brought love and support.

Another scary step forward I faced was learning how to create video content. My first Facebook LIVES were awful! If you're in this space, what I want to tell you is, don't worry; everybody's first videos are horrid. Do it anyway! You will only improve with repetition. Going live helps people get to know you, the real you, behind all the text posts and emails. I created a lot of valuable video content in the beginning that hardly anyone saw or appreciated, but the practice was invaluable.

Over time, I felt like I had started creating content backward. I had no problem recording my voice for people, but being live on camera brought a lot of fear of judgment with it. I was worried about how my clothes and hair looked. I was worried about what was behind me on screen. I was constantly worried one of the dogs would bark while I was LIVE, or that someone watching would be able to hear a fire truck siren in the background since I live one block away from a fire station. I was worried someone would comment, and I would miss it and not respond while live. I was plagued by worry! Let me just tell you, most people don't give a fuck about any of that as long as they feel like they know and like you.

I was definitely holding back in the first six months, not allowing my true self to shine through on camera. But, again, the more you practice, the more natural it starts to feel. From there, I started creating recorded content for TikTok and Instagram. This was so much easier because I could think about it in advance, record it, and then edit or redo it if needed.

Finally, my guides told me to start a podcast in late 2021. I was like, "What the fuck?" I don't even listen to podcasts myself. But I trusted the internal nudge, and I did it. I wanted to keep it simple. While out jogging on nature trails, I realized incredible ideas for a podcast for moms would come to me. I wondered how I could remember them to record them later. I said, "Screw it," and I looked into apps I could use to record my voice out in nature, and then I just started doing it!

So, yes, you can hear birds chirping, bicycles going by, or airplanes in the background, but I decided to embrace it being messy. In fact, I deliberately make the podcast episodes imperfect. I do not edit them in any way. I believe the world needs to see and hear more real, more imperfect, especially moms.

So, if you are uncomfortable in front of a camera, you might start with a podcast, move your way to recordings, and then finally go LIVE. You're going to make mistakes! No need to be mortified. See each one as a gift, a lesson to learn from, and as they happen, ask, "What didn't work?" "How can I do it differently next time?" Embrace your mistakes, learn from them, and then let them the fuck go.

No BS Biz Tip #5

Another lesson I learned on my path is that **comparison is rarely beneficial**. Wise words from one of my spiritual guides that helped me with this are, "There can be no acceptance with comparison. Let go of comparison to find acceptance." You are not like anyone else. There's no reason to copy others or compare yourself. You aren't meant to imitate; you are meant to create. You are unique. Just be YOU!

2022 has taught us, as entrepreneurs, you have to be ready to shift. The world has changed dramatically. Many people's beliefs and income have pivoted. What you are offering as a program, product, service, or coaching service may no longer resonate for you or your clients. That's okay. There's nothing wrong with allowing your business to transform alongside you, which is exactly what I'm doing.

No BS Biz Tip #6

Many people fucking hate change, but it's the one and only constant in life. Accepting it and going with the flow will make everything so much easier. What I originally wanted to offer clients was so limited compared to what I now know I can do and bring to the world. **Don't limit yourself!**

One of the biggest lessons that I've learned this last year is that I don't *HAVE* to listen to anyone. I don't have to follow someone else's advice, no matter how experienced and wealthy they are, if it doesn't resonate with me. Most coaches or mentors are teaching you from their style, their point of view. They teach you what worked for them. Their success came from their energy, so copying them is not going to automatically give you 5 figure months! So now, when I listen to the coaches and experts I follow, I reflect on their advice, and then I decide if it resonates with me and my values.

No BS Biz Tip #7

Make your business your own. Do it your way! It will feel better. I continue on my journey within, finding myself and taking care of myself in a way I never have before. This transformation affects everything around me, including my business, which continues to evolve.

I am currently holding space to explore how my natural healing skills and my spiritual gifts will combine to help my clients. I know there is so much more I can offer women to help them heal, release, and find joy. The magic is ready to be mother-fucking-birthed! I trust what the Universe is unfolding for me.

Michelle Jones-Dauberman

No BS Empowerment

Do you want the No BS path to entrepreneurship? Then be prepared to throw away everything you know or have been taught. I am an empowerment coach, as my "short title," but the truth is that I am a NO BS EMPOWERMENT COACH. I don't have the time for people who are *wishie-washie* with wanting change in their life or business. This isn't said to be mean or unsympathetic. I say it because that was me, full of BS excuses. I let excuse after excuse justify why I was not moving forward in my life and business:

- *Mom hates me.*
- *My Dads don't want to be bothered with me.*
- *My husband cheats, hides things from me, and disrespects me.*
- *My children are taking up all my time and energy, and money.*

- *People online are mean to me.*
- *I'm disrespected.*
- *My feelings got hurt.*
- *I'm broke.*
- *I'm misunderstood.*
- *My beloved coaches just don't get me.*

I could go on and on.

The truth is, *Butterfly*, you most likely have used real-world problems to justify not moving forward, just as I did. I get it, and I see you. The issues are real; however, the reasons for not acting to make a change are BS, and I just told you, I'm a *No BS EMPOWERMENT COACH*. So, let's cut the shit and get to the heart of all the mess…

No BS Biz Tip #1

You get to create the business or life YOU want on YOUR TERMS. First, **choose what the hell you want your life and business to *really* look**

like. Get detailed as you journal out what the perfect life for you is. Some helpful prompts:

- Where are you living?
- What are you doing day to day in this life? Who is sharing it with you?
- What treatment will you not accept?
- What standards will you hold *YOURSELF* to?
- If you are calling in a partner, what attributes do you want them to have?
- What does your business look like?
- How does your ideal client show up?
  - Do you have to convince them to buy, or are they ready?
  - Do clients pay promptly, or do you have to chase them for payments?
  - Are clients open to communication, or do they make excuses?
- What are your hours of operation?
  - You still want family time.

- What time zones are you willing to work with?
- What days will you be closed?
- What times will you respond to messages or emails?
- What are your payment processors?
- What type of payment plans will you offer?
- What holidays will you be closed?
- When will you schedule your vacation?

I spent two months writing 'til my fingers hurt trying to get clear on what my desired path looked like. I still revisit this often to tweak it as I go. As I share this with you, I think of all the clients I worked with who refused to journal out their thoughts about what it is they wanted out of life, and I see them *all* stuck still. I don't want that for you, *Butterfly*, so… *WRITE IT OUT!*

No BS Biz Tip #2

Having boundaries around your time and energy is so important. After all, most places of business have hours of operation, and they don't care if it's inconvenient for you. I didn't do this early on, and it showed up to bite me in the ass. Set this up early so you won't have this hurdle to crawl over later. You have to have an idea of what you want before you can achieve it.

No BS Biz Tip #3

Second, **be coachable *BUT* take responsibility for how *YOU* want your business or life to look.** A while back, I told my coach that I wanted to do a 30-day Facebook LIVE challenge. The purpose of that challenge for me was to introduce myself to the world and overcome my fear of going live on camera. My coach got excited and said that when I went live to make sure that I included information about my business, and to sell my offer. I became overwhelmed and felt misunderstood because selling wasn't what I wanted to do with this challenge. I shut down and didn't do the challenge at all.

Do you want to know what that got me? *WASTED TIME!* That's what I got for not speaking my truth. I don't blame my coach for this. They were simply doing what they thought best and only had my best interest at heart. I love this coach and would recommend them to anyone. The blame is on *ME* for not clearly explaining my desire for my business, my personal experience, and my personal development. I am responsible for this; when we recognize that taking personal responsibility is the only way to create our lives intentionally, the game changes. Sovereignty is key!

When we take responsibility for all the good and all the bad in our lives, we then have the power to change it. Your coach and your clients can't help you or see you if you are not willing to voice what you need, your goals, or what that path looks like for you! It's like any other relationship; if you can't voice what you need in the relationship, then the chances of getting those needs met greatly diminish.

I know now that if I am willing to shut down when presented with a strategy that doesn't align with my ideas, then I have deeper work to do. *Much deeper.* Keep this in mind, *Butterfly.* The power is you!

Think about your experiences in the working world. What didn't serve you? Next, think about what you want from your business. For example, if working holidays were something you didn't enjoy while working in the corporate world, then you shouldn't be doing it in your business.

Years ago, I worked as a virtual assistant (VA) for a coach that, at the time, I truly admired and was completely infatuated with, who was a self-made millionaire and someone I perceived to be a badass, like myself. That is, until I was expected to answer texts and be available at all times. I watched my idol fall with message after message. She was clocking in more hours as a VA than I did as a store manager in my old corporate world job. I watched her become everything I didn't want to be as a coach. For that, I am grateful for the experience. I share this because it's important that you know what your business looks like for you so that you communicate that with whomever you are working with and maintain those boundaries.

No BS Biz Tip #4

Running a no BS business means sharing who you are with the world. Your social media profiles need to state who you are and who you serve. If you are serious about having a business, then shout it out to the world. Stop hiding in fear of what your family or friends will say. **Fear is what holds most entrepreneurs back.**

Fear of judgment.
Fear of failure.
Fear of success.
Fear for the sake of being afraid.

Remember this: the opinions of sheep don't matter to the wolf.

In my second marriage, I was afraid of my husband leaving me. Afraid I wouldn't be able to raise my daughters on my own. It wasn't until I realized he was never home, he was never helping me, and in the end, I was the only breadwinner, that I clearly saw that my fear of failing as a single mom was unfounded. I was already doing the things I was afraid I wouldn't be able to do on my own.

All your fears are unfounded when you really look them in the face. These people that you are holding back for won't create the life you want for you. Only you can do that.

No BS Biz Tip #5

At the time of this publication, Facebook, LinkedIn, and Instagram are the most used social media platforms for business growth. Are you using them fully to your advantage? Do your bios clearly state who you are, unapologetically? Does your profile show a photo of you or a puppy? The puppy is cute, I love puppies, but your clients need to see you. *YOU* **are the face of your business…*SHOW IT*!** A no BS business owner wants to be seen!

No BS Biz Tip #6

Does your cover photo show what you do clearly? Do you have your links listed? Linktree.com makes this easy as pie for folks to find you and your products. **Test your links regularly**. Working as a VA, I can't tell you how many times I would click on links that were broken, and these coaches were wondering why they were not getting web traffic. Broken links lead to no sales! Period!

No BS Biz Tip #7

Make sure you are posting about your business! Verizon, ATT, Walmart, hell, even toilet paper companies are not afraid to boast their wares everywhere… all the time! *Why shouldn't you?* Anyone getting annoyed at your business posts is not your ideal client anyway, so why should it matter? You can always warn your friends and family that you are now using your social media profiles for your business, that these posts are important to you, and that they always have the choice to mute you or remove you online if it bothers them.

No BS Biz Tip #8

Make your profile public. How do you expect others to know what you have to offer if your profile isn't set to public? Stop using fear of being seen as the reason you are not at the top! As a VA, I saw it all the time, followed by the entrepreneur I was working for asking, "Why isn't my audience growing?" If your profile isn't public, they won't find you. Simple. *It's the small things.*

No BS Biz Tip #9

One BIG thing you can do to make a huge change is to stop copying other businesses or influencers. **Authenticity is key, as is taking ownership for yourself.** Dancing half-naked isn't going to work for you if you are not aligned with that way of marketing. Nothing wrong with that marketing if your energy matches it. However, if that's not you at the core, your audience will see it for what it is: *a feeble attempt to be seen.*

Model your content after what you do, not what the trends are, because that's what everyone else is doing. Those trends don't help you stand out, but your authenticity will. Think about it like this… imagine you live in a development where every house looks the same. How do you make your house stand out? You make it different from the others… you get plants you love, lawn ornaments, paint the door a color you love, etc., 'til you make it a representation of who you are!

No BS Biz Tip #10

A "No BS Entrepreneur" doesn't have time to worry about what is trendy. They want their services up front all the time. What does that mean? **Consistency with accountability.** Consistent showing up. Consistent over-the-top customer service. Consistent celebrations of your clients' wins. Consistent marketing that is true to you and your brand! Consistently underpromising and over-delivering.

I also said accountability because a coach can help you decide if what you are doing is working. Being consistent in the wrong thing isn't going to get you results. Having someone to be accountable to helps you decide if a change in wording, marketing, or even branding is needed.

No BS Biz Tip #11

Stop cock blocking your blessings by putting time limits on them. We do this all the time, like when we get down on ourselves, wondering things like, "She made six figures in 30 days… what's wrong with me?"

I know several coaches I could name that had this success and lost it because they were not prepared for the work it takes to maintain it. One coach had that quick success, and in the three years since then, they have changed her business model *four times*, from business coach to TikTok Coach, to Human Design Coach, and now (for now) a sex coach. They couldn't maintain the success.

Slow and steady wins the race. It's great to have a plan. It is great to have goals, but it's better to keep working on that plan and towards those goals consistently rather than constantly changing your mind because you feel like you're missing out. The grass really is not greener on the other side. When you go slow and steady, and that six-figure hits you… then you will be ready for it emotionally. And notice I said "when," not "if."

No BS Biz Tip #12

Remember earlier I said to be coachable? **Make sure you have a coach.** You will need someone in your corner who will help you map out your ideas so that you can turn them into your reality. Communicate clearly with your coach. They have so many ideas and experience in the field, and their minds are at the ready. However, if they give you an idea that doesn't align with your vision, let them know! They always have another plan waiting to be executed.

Keep in mind sometimes you have to challenge yourself and step outside your box to reach that achievement. Don't confuse your coach stretching you and challenging you to grow with unalignment. In my earlier example, my coach was completely right that I must show up and sell my coaching… as uncomfortable as I was with that. They were 100 percent correct!

The unaligned part was my reason for going LIVE at that time. I had a specific purpose for that 30-day FBLIVE challenge, and I should have communicated that better with my coach. Then I could have done another 30-day challenge afterward, at which time I could have offered my services to the public. I shut down so that my problem was bigger than just going LIVE. I had some work in communication that needed doing. Recognizing our triggers helps us grow. Triggers are hints that something needs to be looked into.

No BS Biz Tip #13

If you state, "I love apples. I have studied countless varieties of apples. Apple pies are the best, and I dream of apples all the time," be prepared for someone to tell you that you are wrong and only peaches make the best pies. How do you handle that? Do you doubt your authority now? Is all your research and experiences with apples no longer true because some peach lover wants to be seen and heard? Do you question your in-depth apple knowledge and self-worth? This trigger is called *imposter syndrome,* and *peach lovers* feed off it. They will say something to elicit a reaction from you.

We call them all kinds of names like Armchair Heroes, Trolls, and Keyboard Warriors…. when really they are just people wanting to be seen and heard, and you are threatening their spotlight. I lost a huge amount of time because I let these *peach lovers* take up rent in my space. Space that was meant for *ME!*

They were not paying my bills. Their information was not correct based on my research and experiences. They were not my ideal client. Despite all of that, I let them shut me down. I questioned all my research and training and allowed the word of one nobody to question my faith in myself. Wasted time! Please don't fall for it! It's total BS! Learn about your craft. Never stop learning. Most importantly, remember, "Imposters never worry about having imposter syndrome."

No BS Biz Tip #14

Make sure you are using your time wisely to effectively grow your business. We all have learned early on as children how to *appear* to be busy. I can look as busy as anyone and accomplish absolutely nothing after several hours, and so can you. We relearn how to be busy as a teenager when the manager at the grocery store you are working at tells you, "If you have time to lean, you have time to clean." You learned really quickly that perception matters, and you are never seen by that manager again without a broom in your hand. That manager then thinks you are the busiest employee they have, when in fact, you were just gossiping about Friday night's football game with the grocery bagger!

In business, simply looking busy won't cut it. You have to roll up your sleeves and put in some elbow grease. When working on your business, make sure you are setting goals. *Goals that can be measured.* Maybe it's a block of time that is used specifically to create five days of content. At the end of that block of time, you should be able to measure the output, such as having five days of posts written. Maybe it's 30 minutes dedicated to reading two chapters from a book your coach recommended. That's measurable. Busy work wastes time, and a no BS entrepreneur doesn't have time for waste.

You got this, *Butterfly.* And why do I call you *"Butterfly"*? A butterfly starts out as a caterpillar. Then they it goes through a metamorphosis where they are liquified and reborn as a *butterfly.* They endure so much trauma, and then they become one of the most beautiful creatures in this world, yet they can't see how truly beautiful they are, but everyone else can. People are like that as well. It's my desire that *YOU* know how beautiful you are and that you own your power. Stop letting BS keep you grounded when you are meant to fly. Go fly, *Butterfly*! Show the world your beauty!

Renee Talbot

Heal the World.

It all started when I was about eight years old. Before that, everything is foggy. It was at that young age that my mission and life vision entered my life and heart. I knew I was here to help people heal, feel better, and be authentically free by standing in their own power. I'm here to show others that life can be good, that people can thrive beyond their wildest dreams, that natural is the way to go, and to help people tune to the riches available to them.

When I had this awakening to my purpose, from then on, my nerves were constantly besieged. Land masses have electric and magnetic charges, the air is charged with electricity, the earth's core rumbles and groans… and I could feel it all. The sounds were excruciating. Light, sound, and motion all caused me pain. My body soaked up these energetic waves with no relief in sight.

Stand in my shoes for a moment. Imagine that your nerves are on a hairpin trigger, and everything you feel is amplified by ten times your normal perception. Every day you wake up, it feels like you've been struck by lightning and that you cannot release the energy from your body. Your body is constantly tense, and at night your mind runs in circles, pure chaos, with no rest. Living like this is… *exhausting*.

No BS Tip #1

In the middle of all of this, I lost track of myself, too overwhelmed by feeling everyone else's moods. I felt the pain and symptoms in their bodies, and I became completely detached from my own body. **Because of the pain I endured, at eight, I dreamt of becoming a massage therapist. Often our greatest struggles hint to us at what our soul's purpose is.** I felt that helping people out by kneading and releasing the stress from their bodies would surely fulfill me.

My early school experiences were extremely painful. I grew up living on a native reservation, and I felt very isolated as I didn't fit into the culture. The kids were all in clicks that I wasn't welcomed into. You were not allowed to play any games with anyone unless the leader let you in on a game of tag. This rarely happened. In the classroom, everything in my locker ended up broken, stolen, or scattered around. Even my flute went missing at one point, though luckily, it was returned. The teachers, who at the time were mainly Caucasian, would stand up in the classroom and call us all stupid, and graded us unfairly. On a daily basis, I was ignored or bullied, subject to the whims of the kid who was the *playground king*.

At home, my dad was often gone for music practice, and my mom would be away working. She helped earn the money that put the food on the table. Whenever our family members stopped by for meals, they always wanted something from us.

By middle school, not much had changed. My dad was still gone a lot, and my mom worked. Every Sunday night, there was church to attend. Wednesday nights was youth group. At this time, I still felt like an outsider, a casual observer of this miraculous thing called life. The challenges I faced, the pain, isolation, bullying… you'd think I would have given up on humanity, but instead, it fanned the flame brighter in my heart to improve this world.

When I was old enough, I followed my childhood dream to be a massage therapist when I got older. In 2005, after a year and a half of training and about 700-900 study hours, I graduated. Unfortunately, things didn't work out as well as planned. This ten-year goal had crashed to the ground. I couldn't handle feeling everyone's pain day in and day out anymore. I was shattered. This was one of the only ways I knew to succeed.

I gathered my courage, faced my fears, and asked myself, "Self? How can I truly live my lifelong dreams of helping people live their best lives? How can I truly let my heart lead the way, leaving a positive and hugely impacting legacy of peace in this world? How can I be a truly inspiring beacon, leading people into truly empowered lives?"

No BS Tip #2

By recognizing I wasn't wholly on the right path and asking the right questions, the answer presented itself. **Letting go of our need to control is pivotal to the path to lasting success.** What I discovered was that one portion of the massage course for continuing education credits was *Healing Touch therapy*. Here was a modality that was easily understood and done, without the pain getting stuck and easily returning to the body. Emotions are cleared more quickly. Working at the very roots produces extremely profound results. This made my heart happy; it was finally a real solution!

Shortly after discovering Therapeutic Touch, I was scanning my bookshelf and picked up *The Tapping Cure* by *Roberta Temes*. Lo-and-behold, within the gooey, warm fuzzy inside of this treasure, was a very simple to learn and easy-to-perform healing method. I learned that simply tapping on your acupuncture points could help with smoking, stress, weight loss, and a whole bunch of other things!

I started offering short sessions by text chat for things like increased energy, well-being, and clearing businesses energetically so they could be open to receiving more clients. One of my first ten cases was a gentleman who responded from an African non-governmental organization. We did the basic rounds back and forth, me typing out the points and him doing them. After about forty minutes, he finally broke down, telling me that he'd been pretty much stuck in life for the past two years. His wife had died tragically, and when we'd started our session, he was a 10 on the 1-10 pain scale. After those forty minutes, he was down to a 1-2, took a deep breath, and felt he could move forward in life. For me, it was a profound moment I'll never forget.

No BS Tip #3

That monumental point in my life brought the hands of time to a complete, screeching halt. **When you are on the right path, you'll get clear signs that you are.** From then until now, it has been my mission to help people heal, relax, and *BE* authentically free. I'm fulfilling my purpose by being a bridge between hope, love, and dreams.

Despite the sadness that came from what felt like endless loneliness, I learned a lot from my experiences. I've studied people conscientiously and networked with people for countless hours to understand more about us as humans. This helped me learn how to fit in, as well as how to best help people, and the planet, grow in a positive direction.

It isn't through verbal communication that people experience my gifts; I am an intuitive feeler. Within a session, people experience peace, a sense of self, belonging, and healing. I have learned beyond the chaos to hold that space of peace, so people can *BE* themselves, in timelessness, free to heal. By listening between spaces and worlds, I feel the pain trapped in time, and shine truth, so people become more of who they were truly born to *BE*.

I love people and all life with passion. I truly want to leave behind a massive legacy of growth and self-empowerment. I have helped people with PTSD feel better about living. I helped a person who had a 6-month case of restless leg syndrome, which disappeared in 45 minutes, and it still hasn't returned seven years later.

I've helped numerous businesses clear stuck energy in their foundations so more clients can flow in. I've helped writers who were experiencing writer's block become unstuck. I've helped managers work on a better mindset for R.O.I. Lots of relaxation cases, one of which relaxed so much that her diabetic numbers and sugar levels lowered significantly. I've worked with dogs over a distance for the past ten years as a volunteer. Personally, this work has helped me to find my inner calm and has allowed me to heal my sleeping pattern, taking me down from needing 90 minutes to fall asleep to only 30 minutes. I'm excited now for you to experience the profound healing of tapping for yourself!

Basic Tapping How-To

The Tapping Points

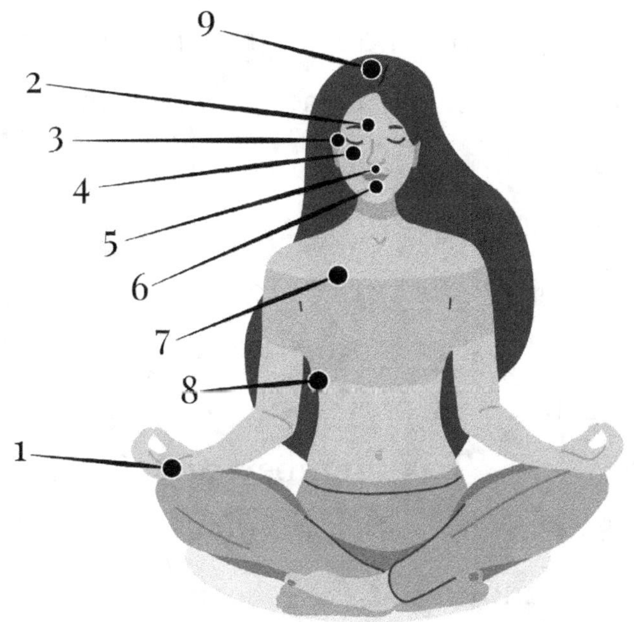

1. Outer side of the hand.
2. Inner eye, Inside the eyebrow.
3. Outside eye by the temple.
4. Under eye, the soft spot under the eye.
5. Under nose.
6. Middle of the chin.
7. Collar bones.
8. Underarm.
9. Top of head.

Before you begin to tap, assess on a scale of 1-10 how much pain you are feeling. Next, begin tapping the various points, starting with the point on the outer side of the hands. Tap 3-or-more times on each point. As you tap, you will speak aloud, or say in your mind, statements or questions that help to your process your physical or emotional pain. You will repeat this process while fully breathing until you can re-rate your pain or emotion at preferably a 1, and re-rate the problem 1-10. The number should have gone down. Each round of tapping the points should take about a minute.

Tapping Scripts:

Open to receiving:

- I'm open to receiving.
- No, are you joking?
- Open to receiving.
- You've got to be kidding me.
- I can do this.

- Really? Just because you think you can…
- Who do you think you are?
- You're joking, there's no way…
- All this remaining receiving.
- Not open, choose receiving.
- Not open, there may be a chance.
- Not open, still honor my journey.
- Getting all goodness, abundance.
- Everything is so clear, I call it in… Abundance rains into my path. Everywhere I look, I see plenty. I accept all available riches.

Walk in Joy:

- Spread peace.
- Arms outreached.
- I become all abundance. I Forgive myself for playing small.
- I am empowered to receive overflow. All paths are peace.
- I align myself with goodness. I reject poorness. I reject greed.

- I give freely.
- Riches resound in my path.

Attracting and creating clients:

- I attract perfect clients.
- You must be joking.
- I attract perfect clients.
- I create soul tribe clients.
- In your dreams.
- I want to create.
- I can create.
- In your dreams.
- I create abundant clients. Only in your dreams!
- Clients I create, clients flow freely.
- I align to their frequency. They are happy to pay me. I am the lighthouse.
- Clients flow in!
- No one comes my way.
- You must be joking.
- Laughing at your efforts.

- 3,2,1 Where are they?
- I am waiting.
- Still waiting.
- Any day now.
- I whistle.
- You believed they'd be.
- So, WHERE?
- I choose creation.
- I welcome my perfect people.
- I expect my perfect tribe.
- They will pay me!
- They come effortlessly.
- I am a master of my skill.
- Deserve nothing but the best.
- Peace, the process works, peaceful pathways forward. I shine bright, brighter!
- My perfect see me, and they come, they are here.
- I am safe achieving my dream.
- I choose safety over fear.

- Open to speaking the truth, my heart is free.
- My mind, soul, and spirit are aligned; my feet follow. It flows. I rest in peace. Everything comes my way easily.
- Lightening the heart.
- I let joy lighten my heart, I let peace hold my heart, I let love embrace my heart, and my heart embraces my body.
- My body tames my mind.
- Light lightens my heart. I dance in joy. I live in joy.
- Joy flows through my soul and DNA. Less junk is holding me down.
- Hope rises. Hope leads. Hope heals.
- What if I doubt? What if I echo these words and they're false?
- I will trust they are real and that the universe has my back.

Tony Babcock

Cut The Crap

Entrepreneurship is often glamorized as a path to financial freedom and independence, but let's be real: *it's not for the faint of heart.* I know this firsthand because I've been there, done that, bought the t-shirt, and guess what? It's one of the old, ratty T-shirts, with a hole in the armpit and a mustard stain on the front… but I love it! From growing up as a queer kid to struggling with self-doubt and imposter syndrome in my entrepreneurial endeavors, I've learned a thing or two about cutting the crap and finding success. So, buckle up, grab some popcorn, and let's dive in.

Growing up gay in a small farm town, I never felt like I fit in. I spent most of my time trying to be like everyone else, the kind of person I thought was tolerable to society. It sucked! It also led to constant people-pleasing, anxious attachment, fear of abandonment, and validation seeking. To this day, I still consider these attributes to be the source of my greatest challenges when it comes to all areas of my life. They're also a double-edged sword in many ways because although they brought, and still bring, a lot of needless suffering, pain, and abandonment trauma, they've also made me the caring, kind, and empathetic human I am today.

I always knew I was meant to help people. Maybe it was my painful beginnings or my affinity for making a difference, but I was always the one who people depended on and came to with their challenges. Nothing quite lit me up like helping someone tap into the light within themselves. This affinity was first facilitated through acting. I stepped onto my first stage at four years old. As the warm lights hit my face and I stepped into the imaginative world around me, I could feel the audience reacting and being moved by my words, actions, and feelings. This was my first taste of standing in my power.

As I followed my acting dreams to *the big city* of Toronto, and eventually to New York City, I continued pursuing this passion on bigger stages and screens and fell in love with the art form even more. *But wait!* Remember that double-edged sword thing? Well, it turns out that acting also enabled some of my bad habits. The constant auditioning reinforced this idea of having to constantly prove myself, seeking validation from others. The ungodly hours and expectations of the industry turned me even more into a people-pleaser. The rejection constantly triggered my abandonment trauma.

Acting was, for all intents and purposes, the best of times and the worst of times for me. It played a pivotal role in my journey early on, my inner journey to self-acceptance. Eventually, I woke up to the fact that I would spend more time and reap more joy from helping actors in the waiting room at auditions, than actually wanting to go into the audition room myself. This led me to open an acting studio that helped actors to become more instinctive and inventive in their work through using the power of improvisation. What followed was 13 years of incredible breakthroughs, and ultimately a huge discovery: what I was *really* doing was helping people uplevel their mindset.

No BS Biz Tip #1

Fast forward to my entrepreneurial journey and opening my corporation, The Present You Inc., to help self-starters and aspiring biz owners stop the negative self-talk shitstorm and run a business that is a creative expression of their integrity and passion. One thing I noticed as I continued to uplevel in my own life? **The struggle and rejection doesn't go away.** In fact, it gets even more difficult. I've had my fair share of both, but instead of staying in the shit, I've learned to use those experiences to fuel my determination and resilience. Every "no" or "failure" is just another opportunity to learn and grow.

No BS Biz Tip #2

Let's be real: entrepreneurship can be a bit of a circus. From the endless meetings to the never-ending to-do lists, it's easy to get bogged down in the day-to-day grind. That's where my sassy, no BS attitude came in handy. I didn't have time for anyone's bullshit anymore, and I sure as hell didn't have time for my own. **If something wasn't working or wasn't adding value, I cut it out.** No questions asked. I didn't have time to waste on things or people that weren't putting me into alignment to reach my goals.

No BS Biz Tip #3

It was scary; it can be really isolating standing in the truth when everyone and everything around you just wants to hype the BS. But it's a necessary journey, one that eventually led me back into the world of Amanda Rose, my amazing biz partner, and we formed the No B.S. Biz Co. on these very principles. *Cut the shit, stand in your truth, and take massive action so that you can blast through all the BS that is EVERYWHERE.*

No BS Biz Tip #4

When I sit and connect the dots between that anxious queer kid trying to be loved and the business powerhouse I am today, I realize something really important: **time is the most precious commodity in life, especially as an entrepreneur.** I couldn't afford to waste it on things that weren't going to move the needle forward. Many people don't understand this, which is why I had to set bulletproof boundaries around my time and how I spent it.

It wasn't just about cutting out the things that weren't working, either. It was also about being laser-focused on my goals and my vision. I knew where I wanted to go, and I made sure that everything I did was aligned with creating that vision, so that if anything felt out of integrity, it got dealt with ASAP. Don't get me wrong. This does not mean I walk around with zero compassion; quite the opposite. It's that now the compassion starts with me. I stopped trading my self-worth for validation, and I realized that the only true way to be fulfilled, which has nothing to do with getting material stuff, by the way, is to *DO ME*.

No BS Biz Tip #5

You Do You. That is the mantra I lead with now. It's fun and funny, yes, but it's also deeply powerful and profoundly simple. If you want to live your life at the highest frequency, you must do YOU first. You must do things YOUR way. This is what cutting the shit is all about. What exactly is the *shit*? It's all of the *things*, people, circumstances or otherwise, that are keeping you from seeing your most authentic, powerful self.

No BS Biz Tip #6

Our job as entrepreneurs is to hold up a mirror to the world so we can help people work through challenges. That always starts with us. Looking back, I see my journey was all about this discovery. It wasn't always easy. I'm certainly not done growing or learning, and there were times when I had to make tough, heart-breaking decisions and say no to opportunities that weren't the right fit, despite a ton of heartache. Ultimately, I knew that staying true to my vision was more important than chasing every shiny object that came my way, which was and is still hard, especially with diagnosed ADHD.

No BS Biz Tip #7

One of the biggest lessons I learned along the way was the importance of taking risks. **Risk = Reward, every time,** even if it takes a hell of a long time for the reward to show up. As an entrepreneur, you're constantly faced with uncertainty and ambiguity, but if you want to succeed, you have to be willing to take risks and step outside of your comfort zone, time and time again.

I cannot begin to underscore enough the value of building relationships and surrounding myself with people who support and believe in me. I couldn't have done it alone, and I'm grateful for the people who have been with me on this journey.

No BS Biz Tip #8

Perhaps the most important lesson I learned was the power of perseverance. There were so many times when I felt like giving up and when I didn't know how I was going to make it through another day. When I laid on the floor of my acting studio while it was metaphorically falling out from underneath me, in mountains of debt, sobbing for hours, it would have been easy to have thrown in the towel. But I kept going. I refused to give up on my dreams, and I refused to let one challenge derail everything I worked for. That's what ultimately led me to success. I didn't give up. I kept pushing forward, even when shit hit the fan. I stayed true to myself and my vision, and I worked my ass off to make it a reality.

The moral of my story? Being an entrepreneur isn't easy. It takes hard work, dedication, excruciating pain tolerance at times, and a huge helping of the scariest ingredient: facing yourself. It's also one of the most rewarding things you can do. If you're willing to take risks, stay true to yourself, and cut the crap, you can achieve anything you set your mind to.

Maybe one day you will look back and realize that all those tough times were just stepping stones to something greater. That your inner child is actually your best asset and greatest teacher and that your flaws are what make you powerful. This all comes with a commitment to finding the truth, your truth, no matter how painful.

No BS Biz Tip #9

Here are a few practical steps you can take to cut the crap in your biz:

1. **Identify what's not working:** Take a hard look at your business and identify what's not working. What processes or systems are causing frustration and wasting time? What clients or projects are draining your energy? Once you've identified these things, it's time to cut them out.

2. **Stay focused on your vision:** It's easy to get distracted by shiny objects and opportunities that aren't aligned with your vision. If you want to be successful, you need to stay focused on your long-term goals. Before taking on any new projects or clients, ask yourself if they align with your overall vision for your business.

3. **Be ruthless with your time:** As an entrepreneur, your time is your most valuable resource. Don't waste it on things that aren't moving the needle forward in your business. Set clear boundaries and prioritize your tasks based on their importance.

4. **Take calculated risks:** You can't grow your business if you're not willing to take risks. But it's important to take calculated risks that are aligned with your vision and goals. Do your research, weigh the pros and cons, and make informed decisions.

5. **Surround yourself with supportive people:** Building a successful business is hard work, and it's important to have a support system in place. Surround yourself with people who believe in you as well as your vision and who will lift you up when you're feeling discouraged.

By implementing these steps and adopting a "cut the crap" mentality in your business, you can streamline your processes, stay focused on your vision, and make the most of your time and resources. It won't always be easy, but it will be worth it. So go ahead, cut the crap, and find success on your own terms.

Amanda Rose

You don't get to the top of a mountain with one major leap; you climb a mountain one step at a time.

My first year as an entrepreneur, from July to December 2013, I made a grand total of $600. I had quit my job at the end of June that year and, within a week, started my entrepreneurial journey. I had no idea what I was doing. That first month, July, I made a whopping 60 bucks. This was, mind you, with me throwing myself at it with *everything* I had. Putting in 12-hour days trying to learn and apply online marketing and sales techniques.

Now, frankly... I was damned proud of the $60 I'd made that first month. That income meant something more than the amount it represented. That was money that I made *online from home*. It confirmed to me that it was even possible to do that. As an introvert that can be classified as a hermit, this was huge!

As an 80's baby and a 90's kid, who grew up with a dad who ran his own IT business, I've always loved being on computers. Even when I was quite young, we had multiple home personal computers. This, of course, in the 90's was a rarity.

I loved playing computer games and video games. I loved writing stories and letting my imagination run free in Word Docs. I loved meeting people who shared similar interests, such as anime, PlayStation, or Nintendo, in online chats. I loved getting lost in movies and TV shows. Basically, if it was in front of a TV screen or a computer monitor, I loved it.

I remember, often, during summer break from school, my mother was perplexed about why I would choose to be inside on my computer rather than outside playing in the sunshine. I loved looking out the window at the beautiful trees full of green leaves and drenched in sunlight, but I rarely felt the need to go out in it. As an adult, while I'm now more appreciative of the warm weather, I'll often still opt to remain indoors, much to the bemusement of my husband and other people who know me. Additionally, I can go over a month without leaving the house, and often do, with a whole heap of gratitude to my husband, who lovingly gets in any necessities we need. I really mean it when I say that I'm a hermit.

No BS Biz Tip #1

All this to say, if there was a chance I could work from home, on a computer, and earn enough money doing it, I was all-in to figure that out. This was the most soul-nurturing way to make a living that I could imagine! **Your natural inclinations are something you should listen to.** Life isn't meant to be a never-ending struggle. Where you feel the most nurtured, inspired, and happy, these are major indicators of the path you should be pursuing to bring the most joy and fulfillment into your life.

In those first few weeks, months, and years, I failed constantly. Multiple times daily. In fact, I'm pretty sure I found new ways to fail that nobody had ever discovered. But I didn't care. I needed it to work more than I needed to save my ego from being bruised. I got curious about the failures and why what I had tried didn't work. On the flip side, the rare time that something I did actually yielded results, I then had a new tool in my toolbox to use.

No BS Biz Tip #2

Failure needs to be embraced. You're only growing when you're challenging yourself to grow. Inevitably, when we try something new, we're likely to fuck it up before we figure it out. As adults, we tend to avoid doing anything outside of our comfort zones. We play small. We let our fear dissuade us from going after our dreams. That has to end.

Kids throw themselves at new opportunities to grow and express themselves. Think about a toddler that's learning to walk. Do they get it right on the first try? Of course not! They fall down, but they get up again and keep trying until they get it right. No parent sees their child give their first attempt at walking, then fall, and declares, "Well, I guess little Johnny just isn't going to be a walker." That would be absurd! It is likewise absurd to think that just because you don't hit a home run on your first try that you won't be able to eventually get it. Practice makes perfect.

As I continued to fumble, fall, and get back up, it was an exciting and exhausting journey. It was tooth and nail for years as I learned the ropes, and thankfully, my husband's job at the time, although just a smidge over minimum wage, gave me the space to keep trying. Living under the poverty line, year after year, was quite difficult, but the idea of going back out into the workplace just wasn't an option in my heart.

No BS Biz Tip #3

In my second year in business, I made roughly $2000. The third year was about $3600. It was painstakingly slow growth. Despite the time it took, I was determined that success was inevitable. **You have to believe that you can do it.**

No BS Biz Tip #4

I continued learning, growing, and implementing. It wasn't easy. Even though in my heart I believed in my success, there was doubt and fear, and frustration. Outwardly, when you look at other people, their success seems radically fast. In fact, people tell me all the time how fast things came to me, but the reality is that it's been slow. **It's through consistent daily action, in spite of fear, in spite of doubt, in spite of the million reasons to quit, that you keep your**

eyes on your goal, and you keep fucking going. You don't climb a mountain in one outrageously high leap; you do it one step at a time.

In 2016 my husband lost his job, and everything changed. That year I was earning about $600-1000 a month, and while that had been a huge leap forward from previous years, it certainly wasn't enough to pay our mortgage, car payments, utilities, feed us, etc. I was terrified. I couldn't face ever going back to work for anyone else ever again. So, I did the one thing I'd been avoiding... I turned inward.

No BS Biz Tip #5

Rock bottom can be the best opportunity you ever get to make lasting changes. When there's next-to-nothing left to lose, when you're faced with some serious real-life consequences for not changing, you can find an immense power within that you didn't know you had. You can face your fear head-on; in fact, you have to. There's no escaping it.

Hitting an all-time low is a blessing in disguise. It places you at a crossroads where you get to make a decision. Do you let everything fall apart, or do you remember that you're a fucking warrior, that you create your life, that there's nothing on heaven or earth that can stop you when you set your mind to do something? I faced that crossroads, and I chose the latter. I hope, should you find yourself in that position, you remember what a powerful badass you really are.

When you choose to tap into the true power that's within you, there's nothing that can stand in your way. You'll do whatever it takes. You'll lose every excuse you have, and you'll do those damn things, no matter how out-of-your-comfort-zone they are.

No BS Biz Tip #6

I dove into reading every book I could get my hands on about money mindset and manifestation. I embodied all the woo. Strategy had only gotten me so far, and I had a hollering in my soul that told me that mindset was the key to reaching the next level, and holy shit, was that inkling ever right! Mindset is everything. **Master your mindset, and you master your life.**

It was a challenging 6-months that followed that tested me emotionally, mentally, and spiritually. There isn't anything easy about facing your fears head-on; it's why most people never do. Luckily, my desire for change overrode my egoic self-imposed limitations. At the end of it, after nearly a decade of living under the poverty line, we manifested over 6-figures. Our lives radically changed.

In the following years, I have had the pleasure of bringing many lifelong dreams to life. I built my corporation, The Infinite Power of

You INC., and Co-Founded No BS Biz Co. Ltd. With Tony Babcock. I became a Business, Wealth, Manifestation, and Mindset Coach, a Multi-Published Multi-Genre Author with over 20 publications out and more on the way, a Motivational Speaker, and a Course Creator with over 40 life-transforming programs out so -far. In 2021 my husband and I moved into our dream home.

I've been featured in many publications and news articles for my work, including FOX, CBS, Yahoo! Finance, and NBC, and I was recently recognized with the BRAINZ Global 500 Award and the CREA 2021 Award. And, in 2022, I became a Self-Made Millionaire. I live to fulfill my mission of shifting human consciousness to create soulful abundance through mindset practices. *I live my life on my terms.*

No BS Biz Tip #7

You can do anything. You can accomplish anything. It's not an overnight change. You're redefining who you are to build your dreams. **Embrace the journey.** You got this!

MEET THE AUTHORS

Erin Nettere

Erin Nettere is the founder of Soultivity Studio, a digital marketing agency specializing in soulful social media strategy. Through her work at Soultivity Studio, she empowers her team and clients to find their true voice in a noisy social space while achieving their business goals through mindful strategies. Her goal is to help entrepreneurs shine and find their dream clients, all while transforming their relationship with social media and turning it into an act of self-care.

Throughout her career, she has built up many accounts to help them achieve their goals of growth and notoriety working with their dream brands; Burts Bees, Mind Body Green, and The Discovery Channel, in addition to book publishers and other print publications, to name a few. She has also helped countless business owners find joy and ease while navigating social media through her coaching program and eBook social media as Self Care for Entrepreneurs. She believes dreams are meant to come true and will do whatever it takes for her and her clients to live their dream lives.

Special Offer: 75% off a deep dive call with Erin: https://soultivity-studio.mykajabi.com/offers/zsfYp2zw/checkout?coupon_code=75OFF

Detoxing your social media:

https://soultivitystudio.com/detoxifyyoursocialmedia

Tony Babcock

Tony Babcock is the CEO and founder of The Present You Inc. and co-founder of the No BS biz Co. Ltd. He is a Certified Life Coach, NLP Practitioner, Author & Speaker. He has worked with over 1500 Creative Entrepreneurs and some of the world's largest companies (including Microsoft), inspiring lasting change & growth from the inside out. He is also a professional actor, TV Host & Entrepreneur with five successful businesses.

Visit:

www.thepresentyouinc.com

Amanda Rose

Amanda Rose is the CEO and founder of The Infinite Power of You INC., Co-Founder of No BS Biz Co. Ltd., a Business, Wealth and Mindset Coach, Multi-Published Multi-Genre Bestselling Author, Motivational Speaker, Course Creator, Actor, and Self-Made Millionaire. Her corporation serves entrepreneurs worldwide, with her unique approach that focuses on understanding each client's individual strengths and guiding them in building their own methodology, rather than attempting to get them to adapt to a specific mold.

Amanda has been a sales expert for over a decade, having experience in door-to-door sales, retail, live sales presentation, network marketing, and online product and service sales, which allows her to bring extensive insight to her clients. Amanda has been featured in many publications and news articles for her work, including **FOX**, **CBS**, Yahoo! Finance, and **NBC**. She was recently recognized with the BRAINZ Global 500 Award and the CREA 2021 Award. Amanda passionately works to help entrepreneurs succeed through her Corporation as well as within her Facebook Community.

Visit:

https://amanda-rose.mykajabi.com/

Becky Shapiro

JOY has become MF elusive for most, especially moms. For her clients, Becky Shapiro offers self-care, healing, and techniques to let go of resistance to provide direction in rediscovering JOY. As a Mind-Body-Spirit Coach, she empowers you to let go of what's no longer serving you to allow space for what will.

Working with Becky will be a journey, a discovery, and a transformation, leading you to the path that lights you up. Her guidance consists of 1:1 Coaching and/or Healing sessions, an online membership for moms, Journey to Joy, and online courses and classes. She is currently exploring her spiritual and psychic gifts, which will enhance her client sessions, bringing greater clarity and speed to healing and transformation.

Visit:

heartandsoulcompass.com

Special Offer: To receive 25% off all Becky's courses and offers, email Becky at: contact@heartandsoulcompass.com to redeem.

Amy Dabrush Lewis

Nothing inspires Amy more than helping determined entrepreneurs connect deeply with themselves, gain clarity and create consistent cash flow without sacrificing their health or their relationships.

Amy spent over two decades in the fitness business industry. She built multiple 6 figure businesses and helped others do the same in a variety of industries, in addition to consulting with multiple 6-and-7-figure businesses to simplify operations and increase impact and income while changing the workplace/world culture.

With a strong background in sales and marketing, Amy generated award-winning sales to the tune of over a million dollars in less than nine months.

Amy has a passion for helping determined entrepreneurs deeply connect with themselves to create consistent cash flow month over month, quickly, so that they are connected to something greater than themselves, feel supported, and are able to meet and exceed their goals and instigate true change.

She understands that how you do anything is how you do everything, which is exactly why the connection with self is so important.

Amy strives to grow her business with the same integrity, communication, and collaboration that she and her team use with their clients to encourage compassion, expansion, and real results for all.

Website:

www.fusionfitnessvt.com

Social Media:

www.facebook.com/groups/strongbeautifulu/

www.facebook.com/amy.dabrush.lewis/

www.facebook.com/fusionfitnessvt/

www.instagram.com/amylewissolutions

Michelle Jones Dauberman

Michell Phoenix is an empowerment and transformation accountability coach who supports her clients to master their emotions and amplify their fire, allowing them to live life on their terms, creating empowered relationships, life, and business success, living a rejection-proof life and living unapologetically in integrity with their standards of conduct.

Michelle has been featured on the RadAF podcast, the Wylde Life Podcast, and The Infinite Power of You Blog. She dedicates her life to helping one million people, who, in turn, will help millions more create a huge ripple of healing and self-acceptance in the world.

Connect with Michelle:

www.facebook.com/michelle.jonesdauberman

Special offer: Mention "NO BS BOOK" when you reach out to Michelle to receive 40% off your first purchase!

Renne Talbot

Renee Talbot is the founder of A Brilliant Blessing LLC. She is a healer who helps her clients through the power of tapping.

Visit:

www.facebook.com/abrilliantblessingsllc

Kaeli Mulvaney-Courtois

Kaeli Mulvaney-Courtois is a vortex of energy that, when focused in one direction, can shed light on the most difficult of problems. She has experience in a broad range of topics from the arts to the sciences, has teaching qualifications, and maybe a little too good at fitting things into her schedule. Kaeli is an enhancer. A "mechanic" entrepreneur who works behind the scenes, spending her time creating techniques and problem-solving to ensure her clients can be effective, efficient, and who they genuinely are.

There is a *METHOD to her MADNESS*, and she can help you find yours as well.

WAYS TO WORK WITH KAELI

- 1:1 session: We can brainstorm, identify hurdles, problem solve, test out methods for efficiency and effectiveness, fix scheduling, etc.
- Business Analysis: The basic steps include allowing me to explore and learn all about your business and how it runs. I ask a lot of questions! We identify struggle areas and spend time testing solutions to find the best fit for your business and the people that work in it. Put those methods into place and watch your business become more effective and efficient, allowing you to be able to do more with what you have.

Connect:

www.facebook.com/kaeli.courtois